stronomy

ool Women in Space

GIRLS IN SCIENCE

Anita Yasuda

Illustrated by
Lena Chandhok

Nomad Press
A division of Nomad Communications
10 9 8 7 6 5 4 3 2 1

This book was manufactured by Marquis Book Printing,
Montmagny Québec, Canada
August 2015, Job #114417
ISBN Softcover: 978-1-61930-330-0
ISBN Hardcover: 978-1-61930-326-3

Illustrations by Lena Chandhok
Educational Consultant, Marla Conn

Questions regarding the ordering of this book should be addressed to
Nomad Press
2456 Christian St.
White River Junction, VT 05001
www.nomadpress.net

Printed in Canada.

~ Other Title in the **Girls in Science** Series ~

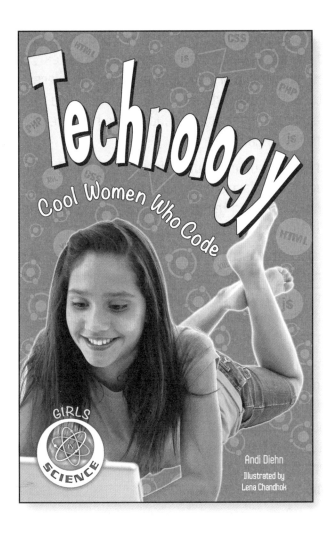

HOW TO USE THIS BOOK

In this book you'll find a few different ways to further explore the topic of women in astronomy.

The essential questions in each Ask & Answer box encourage you to think further. You probably won't find the answers to these questions in the text, and sometimes there are no right or wrong answers! Instead, these questions are here to help you think more deeply about what you're reading and how the material connects to your own life.

There's a lot of new vocabulary in this book! Can you figure out a word's meaning from the paragraph? Look in the glossary in the back of the book to find the definitions of words you don't know.

Are you interested in what women have to say about astronomy? In the She Says boxes you'll find quotes from women who are professionals in the astronomy field. You can learn a lot by listening to people who have worked hard to succeed!

Primary sources come from people who were eyewitnesses to events. They might write about the event, take pictures, or record the event for radio or video. Why are primary sources important?

Interested in primary sources?
Look for this icon.

PS

Use a QR code reader app on your tablet or other device to find online primary sources. You can find a list of URLs on the Resources page. If the QR code doesn't work, try searching the Internet with the Keyword Prompts to find other helpful sources.

CONTENTS

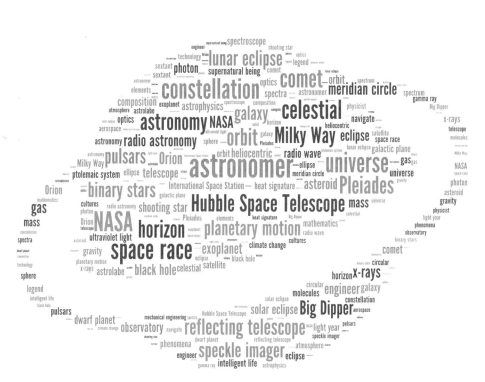

LOOK UP!

When you look up in the clear night sky, you can see the gleaming moon and bright planets of our solar system and a blanket of twinkling stars. Do you ever wonder what lies beyond? What do distant galaxies look like? Imagine using technology so advanced that it allows you to look deep into space at galaxies billions of light years from Earth. You might see stars brighter than our sun being born, super-massive black holes colliding, and objects never seen before.

Maybe your search will reveal a planet capable of supporting life. Are you ready to explore the universe? This is what astronomers do! In *Cool Women in Space*, you'll read about three fascinating women with a passion for space. Each of them has worked or is working in the field of astronomy.

These women have achieved success in their fields through hard work and determination. They have overcome many challenges to achieve their space dreams.

Astronomer Nancy Grace Roman worked for decades with NASA. She is known to many as the "Mother of the Hubble" because she was so closely involved with the development of the Hubble Space Telescope.

Picture This

The Hubble Space Telescope has allowed us to see very distant objects. Because the light from faraway objects has traveled for billions of years to reach us, we measure their distances from us in light years. This also makes the telescope a time machine. It sends photos back to Earth that allow astronomers to prove and disprove theories. We now know that the universe is almost 14 billion years old! NASA makes images from the Hubble available for everyone to view.

Hubble telescope images NASA 🔍

"What everyone in the astronaut corps shares in common is not gender or ethnic background, but motivation, perseverance, and desire—the desire to participate in a voyage of discovery."

—Dr. Ellen Ochoa, former astronaut and director of the Johnson Space Center

Maggie Aderin-Pocock is a scientist, educator, and presenter on the popular BBC show *The Sky at Night*. She makes astronomy interesting and accessible to many people around the world.

Astronomer and professor Andrea Ghez has been listed as one of the Top 20 scientists in the United States. She researches black holes.

Their careers show us that the sky is not the limit, and neither is space. We'll learn more in this book about what they do and why. But first, let's learn about the amazing science of astronomy that these three women have studied and made their careers.

Ask & Answer

Why is it important that both men and women pursue careers in astronomy? What would the science be like if only one gender worked in it?

Chapter 1

A SHORT STORY ABOUT A HUGE SPACE

The universe is an exciting and mysterious place. The study of space and everything in it, from galaxies to gases, is called astronomy. Astronomy is one of the oldest sciences in the world. The word astronomy comes from the Greek word *astron,* meaning "star," and *nemein,* meaning "to distribute."

People have sought to understand the sky for thousands of years. Long ago, they peered into the night with only their eyes. They saw the moon and some of the planets in our solar system. They saw comets and, of course, many stars. All of these things are called astronomical objects or celestial bodies.

With time, people developed many tools to help them study the sky. An astrolabe is an instrument that was used to measure the height of astronomical objects above the horizon. This helped to determine the location of stars. An observatory is a place where astronomers can observe astronomical objects. Sky maps help to locate objects in space and telescopes enable us to see faraway objects up close.

 With time, people developed many tools to help them study the sky.

Advances in mathematics and in many branches of science also helped astronomers. They began to understand the position, movement, and composition of what they saw in the night sky.

Ask & Answer

If you lived in ancient times, what might you have thought when you saw an eclipse or a shooting star?

Explore!

Have an adventure in the night sky from your back yard! Search online or in a book for a sky chart designed for the naked eye. How many constellations can you find? Can you spot the Big Dipper or the constellation of Orion?

Today, scientists have many sophisticated new tools to help them with their research. These tools are found both in space and on the ground. For example, astronomers have charted more than a billion stars in the Milky Way using the Gaia, a space observatory designed to build a three-dimensional catalog of our galaxy.

In the Milky Way galaxy, where our solar system is located, astronomers estimate there may be up to 400 billion stars! Think about all the objects in our solar system. These include mysterious Pluto and its moons, the many rings of Saturn, thousands of asteroids, and comets that seem to come from nowhere.

 Today, scientists have many sophisticated new tools to help them with their research.

There is much more to discover and learn about space. Who is going to make these discoveries? Maybe it will be you!

FINDING OUR WAY THROUGH THE STARS

On a dark and cloudless night, stargazers travel to areas far from the glow of city streetlamps. Here they can see more than 2,000 stars using just their eyes. Binoculars raise this number to tens of thousands and telescopes can reveal billions of stars. Under the immense canopy of the sky, stars may appear dim and remote. Others are so bright that they look close enough to touch.

Since ancient times, people just like you have regarded the same sparkling bodies of light with awe. Ancient people asked what these objects were. How were they created, and who put them there? They wondered why some stars seemed to travel across the sky while others appeared night after night in the same position.

 Since ancient times, people just like you have regarded the same sparkling bodies of light with awe.

"Reserve your right to think, for even to think wrongly is better than not to think at all."

—Hypatia of Alexandria, early astronomer and mathematician

Science was not developed enough to answer their questions. So people told stories to explain how the universe worked. They gave stars names and grouped them together to form patterns that we now call constellations.

Almost all cultures created myths and legends about celestial bodies. Their stories linked the sun, moon, stars, planets, and other sky phenomena to supernatural beings.

The Inuit of the far north tell of three hunters who, after chasing a bear into the sky, became the three stars in the belt of the constellation Orion. The Assiniboine tribe of the Great Plains speaks of seven brothers transforming themselves into the Pleiades star cluster. The Haida of the Pacific Northwest tell of the Raven, who stole the stars, sun, and moon to transform Earth from a world of darkness to a world of light.

 Almost all cultures created myths and legends about celestial bodies.

Aboriginal groups in Australia tell of the sky woman who creates the morning light with her campfire. As she walks across the sky with her torch, the sun shines on Earth. The day ends when she puts out her campfire. In another aboriginal story, a hunter banishes a giant emu to the sky after it kills his wife, creating the Milky Way.

For thousands of years, astronomers kept records of the skies using bones, cave walls, and clay tablets. People noticed how the sun, moon, and stars moved and found patterns in these movements that they could accurately predict. This is how the entire sky became a map, a calendar, and a clock.

Ancient sailors used the stars to navigate. This helped them to find their way in unknown waters or on the open ocean. Farmers saw which stars appeared overhead at specific seasons. This helped them to know when to plant, irrigate, and harvest crops.

STUDYING THE STARS

The ancient Egyptians were skilled observers of the sky. They knew there were 24 hours in a day. Around 3000 BCE, they used their observations of the celestial bodies to create a calendar with 365 days and 12 months.

HYPATIA

Hypatia was born around 350 CE in Alexandria, Egypt. She was one of the first women to study astronomy. Alexandria was a flourishing city, and home to many scholars. It had a great museum where many important discoveries in mathematics and science were made.

Cave Paintings

This series of interconnected caves was discovered in 1940 by four boys and their dog, Robot. The caves were open to the public to view for several years, but were closed when the paintings began to deteriorate. You can see photographs of the cave painting here. Can you see anything that looks like astronomical objects?

time life Lascaux caves 🔍

The Babylonians were another ancient civilization that studied the skies. They lived in Mesopotamia, a fertile valley between the Tigris and Euphrates rivers. This area is present-day Iraq.

The Babylonians recorded their observations and star charts on clay tablets. They even created tables for predicting solar and lunar eclipses. A solar eclipse is when the moon moves between the sun and the earth. In a lunar eclipse the earth is between the moon and the sun.

Unlike most women of her time, Hypatia was educated. She learned mathematics and astronomy from her father, Theon. Hypatia taught, wrote books, and gave public lectures. Crowds of people came to hear her speak. Sadly, after being accused of witchcraft, she was killed by a mob. Why do you think some people considered her dangerous?

The ancient Chinese believed that the emperor received his authority to govern from the stars. More than 2,000 years ago, Chinese emperors called themselves the "Son of Heaven." An emperor who ruled wisely kept harmony between the earth and the heavens.

Because of this, the role of an astronomer was very important to the Chinese. And, like the Babylonians, the Chinese recorded their observations of the sky, including lunar and solar eclipses and comets.

Back in Egypt, Claudius Ptolemaeus (100–170 CE), known as Ptolemy, claimed that the earth was the center of the universe. In his view, everything in the skies traveled around the earth. Ptolemy's ideas spread across civilizations and were not challenged until the fifteenth century.

Polish astronomer Nicolaus Copernicus lived during the Renaissance, from 1473 to 1543. This was a time of great discovery and scientific growth.

Copernicus was the first astronomer to use mathematics, physics, and astronomy to create a model of the universe. He spent years observing the stars and planets from a cathedral in Frauenburg, Poland. Copernicus challenged the ideas of Ptolemy and changed the way the universe was viewed.

Ptolemy's ideas spread across civilizations and were not challenged until the fifteenth century.

Copernicus believed that the earth was not the center of the universe. Instead, he argued, all planets, including the earth, moved around the sun.

Center of Everything

Until the Renaissance, people believed in the ideas of Ptolemy, called the Ptolemaic system. It stated that the earth was the center of the universe. Take a look at this illustration from 1540. How does it depict this view? Where is the sun in relationship to the earth? What do you think this illustration was used for? Three years after publication, mathematician and astronomer Copernicus challenged this view. Look at the Copernicus model on the same page. How are they different? What would you have thought of this new theory?

Ptolemaic system vs Copernicus system 🔍

Johannes Kepler (1571–1630) continued the work of Copernicus. In his studies of the movement of Mars, he determined that planets move in elliptical orbits around the sun. At the time, it was commonly thought that planets moved in perfect circles.

Kepler explained his discoveries in his three laws of planetary motion. The first law states that each planet moves in an ellipse around the sun. The second law explains that planets move faster the closer they are to the sun. The third law explains the connection between the time it takes a planet to complete its orbit and its distance from the sun.

It was Galileo Galilei (1564–1642) who found evidence to support the theories of Copernicus. Looking through his telescope, Galileo discovered four moons orbiting Jupiter.

CAROLINE HERSCHEL

When Caroline Herschel (1750–1848) was born in Germany, she was expected to either get married and have children or find work as a governess. This was the expectation for most women at that time. But Caroline was lucky. Her father gave her an education.

Caroline's brother, William Herschel, was England's court-appointed astronomer. When she was 22 years old, he trained Caroline to be his assistant and to perform

Galileo's support of the theories of Copernicus made him very unpopular with Roman leaders at the time. In 1633, Galileo was charged with suspicion of heresy, which meant he believed in things most people, and the church, did not believe. He was imprisoned in his house until his death in 1642. Why might a society's leaders reject new ideas? Have you ever held different ideas from people around you?

Galileo's support of the theories of Copernicus made him very unpopular with Roman leaders at the time.

The invention of the reflecting telescope in 1668 resulted in many exciting discoveries. Scientists observed planets, moons, comets, and many other things through equipment that grew more and more advanced with time.

complicated mathematical equations. But Caroline wasn't satisfied to simply help her brother. She also worked at making her own observations.

Caroline was the first woman to be recognized for discovering a comet. Later, she discovered several more comets. When King George III heard about her discoveries, he decided she should be paid for her work. Caroline became the first women in England to hold a paid government job.

FINDING OUR WAY THROUGH THE STARS

Modern scientists have been launching objects into space for half a century. In 1957, the former Soviet Union launched the first artificial satellite into space, called *Sputnik 1*. The success of the launch impressed the world!

Sputnik 1 sparked a surge of new technological and scientific developments, as well as the Space Race. This was not an actual race. It was a rivalry between the Soviet Union and the United States to see which could get to the moon first. In 1968, the United States became the first country to successfully land a person on the moon and return him to Earth. Countries continue to send both people and satellites into space.

Beep!

Sputnik's signal was rebroadcast on the radio. It sounded like a series of beeps, which might not be impressive, but the fact that these beeps were coming from a satellite that humans had sent into space was fascinating to the world. You can listen to the same beeps. What do you think people thought of this sound back in 1957?

Sputnik signal rebroadcast beeps

Going into space is risky. How do space agencies and astronauts decide a mission is worth the risk? How do they make it as safe as possible?

Missions are often joint ventures between many countries. They involve teams of engineers, scientists, technicians, and support personnel. The International Space Station, launched in 1998, was a joint effort between the United States, Russia, Canada, Japan, and the European Space Agency.

NASA and the European Space Agency also worked together on the Hubble Space Telescope. Launched in 1990, the Hubble has made more than a million observations. It still sends spectacular images back to Earth for scientists to analyze. The Hubble has taken the deepest views of space to show, for example, that no two planetary nebulas are alike. A nebula is a cloud of gas or dust that can sometimes be seen at night.

An image from the Hubble

The United States has launched spacecraft such as the *Galileo Orbiter* to study Jupiter and its moons. Robotic rovers on Mars explore where humans cannot yet go. And a NASA space observatory called the *Kepler* is looking for nearby stars that have their own planets.

The universe offers astronomers many challenges. While new discoveries help to unravel mysteries, each discovery seems to create even more mystery.

Ask & Answer

Are you interested in understanding our place in the universe? Do you get excited about Hubble images of other galaxies? Astronomy might be a good career for you.

ASTRONOMY CAREERS

Astronomers do many different things. They use telescopes to take images of astronomical objects. They analyze these images and look for patterns in the data. They make models to test their theories. They also write articles, books, and software.

Astronomers work in government labs or with space agencies, such as NASA. Many work with companies designing and building instruments. You can find astronomers in schools, museums, and planetariums.

Astronomers are scientists who use math and physics to understand and investigate space. They also use tools such as telescopes, satellites, computers, and observatories on Earth and in space.

To be an astronomer, you need to study math and science, learn to work with others, and be able to communicate well. In high school, you can take chemistry, biology, physics, computer science, and advanced math. In college, you will study mathematics, geophysics, and space science.

You can gain experience at local astronomy clubs, planetariums, and space camps. You can also begin your astronomy career at home without any special equipment. Train your eyes by looking for patterns in the night sky. Keep watching, looking, and exploring.

Young Astronomer

Anyone can make amazing discoveries. In 2011, 10-year-old Kathryn Gray was studying astronomical images with her father when she discovered a supernova. A supernova is an exploding star, and astronomers spend hours trying to find them by comparing photographs of the sky taken at different times. Kathryn was persistent, disciplined, and lucky. She became the youngest person ever to find a supernova!

"Kathryn Gray" supernova 🔍

WOMEN IN ASTRONOMY

Women have made important contributions in astronomy since ancient times. In the past, their contributions were often overlooked and their names omitted from history. Today, women are recognized for their scientific work.

Profiles of successful female scientists appear in newspapers, magazines, television programs, and websites. Women win awards and have the same educational opportunities as men. They are able to find positions in astronomy at schools, laboratories, observatories, and space agencies.

In the last decade, according to the American Astronomical Society, the number of women in astronomy has doubled. Every year, female scientists grow in number and provide role models, showing girls that they, too, can explore the universe. Let's meet three women working in space—Nancy Grace Roman, Maggie Aderin-Pocock, and Andrea Ghez.

Get to Work!

You can start now by helping professional scientists, including astronomers, at citizen science websites. Researchers rely on people such as you to help organize and categorize data. It's a lot of fun and great training!

zooniverse 🔍

Chapter 2

NANCY GRACE ROMAN

Does the Milky Way contain all the stars in the universe? This was the question that needed to be answered. In 1925, the largest telescope in the world stood on top of Mount Wilson in California. Scientists were using it to collect data that would prove the existence of galaxies outside the Milky Way. Astronomy would be changed forever! This ground-breaking discovery took place the year Nancy Grace Roman was born.

The Hooker Telescope, the largest telescope in the world in 1925.

The Observatories of the Carnegie Institution for Science Collection at the Huntington Library, San Marino, CA.

From the time that Nancy was a small child, she loved the stars. She learned to recognize constellations and drew pictures of the moon. Later, when Nancy was studying astronomy in school, she described it to a reporter as the "science of where you aren't."

 The long career of Nancy Grace Roman lit a path to the moon, planets, and stars for others to follow.

Nancy earned a graduate degree at a time when few men or women went beyond high school. Her hard work paid off when NASA hired her to create its first astronomy program. There, Nancy oversaw the launch of many observatories. She promoted the building of a space telescope that earned her the unofficial title, "Mother of the Hubble."

Nancy Grace Roman was born in Nashville, Tennessee, on May 16, 1925. She was the only child of Georgia and Irwin Roman. Her mother, Georgia, was a piano teacher. After she married Irwin, Georgia stopped teaching to care for Nancy and run their home.

Irwin was a geophysicist and a professor. He earned his PhD in physics in 1920 from the University of Chicago. A geophysicist studies physical movements of the earth. Months after Nancy was born, the family moved to Oklahoma. They would also live in Texas, Michigan, New Jersey, Nevada, and Maryland.

 Nancy's family moved many times throughout the United States.

Nancy grew up during the Great Depression. This was a time between 1929 and 1941 when the economy in the United States had collapsed. There were lots of people out of work and many families living in poverty. At its worst, almost 25 percent of the workforce in America was unemployed.

Ask & Answer

What do you think Nancy was talking about when she called astronomy "the science of where you aren't?"

Nancy's father was lucky to have a job, even if it meant the family had to move around. From 1931 to 1935, the family lived in Houghton, Michigan, where Irwin worked as an assistant professor of math and physics at the Michigan College of Mining and Technology.

Nancy's mother thought it was important to point out things of interest to Nancy, as many parents do. On some evenings, they admired the sky, looking for constellations and the northern lights. This is how Nancy was first introduced to astronomy.

MARIA MITCHELL

Maria Mitchell (1818–1889) was the first woman astronomer to join the American Academy of Arts and Sciences. Maria opened a school for girls in Nantucket in 1835 and encouraged them to become careful observers of the natural world. She later became the town librarian and used this opportunity to read current works.

In 1847, using her father's telescope, Maria discovered a comet. It was nicknamed "Miss Mitchell's Comet." For her discovery, Maria was awarded a gold medal by the King of Denmark. He had promised to give a medal to anyone who discovered a new comet with a telescope. Maria became a celebrity. She was recognized for her work by the

Later, Irwin joined the Civil Service, working with the U.S. Bureau of Mines and U.S. Geological Survey as their senior geophysicist. The family was on the move again.

THE YOUNG ASTRONOMER

For two years, the Roman family lived on the outskirts of Reno, Nevada. In 1936, Nevada had one of the smallest populations in the United States. The Fleischmann Planetarium and Science Center at the University of Nevada would eventually be built there 30 years later.

American Academy of Arts and Sciences and by the American Association for the Advancement of Science.

In 1865, Maria accepted a position at Vassar College. She became the first female professor of astronomy, not only in the United States, but in the world. After her death in 1889, the Maria Mitchell Society was formed to promote her legacy. You can learn more about Maria's life and explore artifacts from her work. What made her succeed in a field that included so few women at that time? Was it determination, luck, or a combination of both?

"Maria Mitchell" astronomer 🔍

With its clear night skies, the desert in Nevada provided a great view of the stars. They were a constant source of fascination for Nancy. Even today, Nevada is known for having some of the darkest skies in the country, making it a popular destination for stargazers.

During Nancy's second year in Reno, she began an informal astronomy club. A few of Nancy's friends gathered at her home for fun stargazing evenings. It was exciting to search for constellations! At the end of that summer, Nancy was hooked on astronomy.

Seeing Stars

Nancy and her friends used a book called *Seeing Stars* by W.B. White as their guide. Today, there are lots of illustrated books for kids who are curious about the sky, but in the 1930s, this was one of only a handful. The author begins by telling the readers that anyone can be an astronomer. All they need is a sharp pair of eyes. The book contains illustrations and photographs of stars and planets from the Yerkes Observatory of the University of Chicago, where Nancy would later become a student.

You can look at samples from a children's book on space published in 1953. What do you notice that's similar to books you might find in the library today? What's different? Why?

1953 Yerkes Observatory photos

By seventh grade, Nancy was certain that she wanted to become an astronomer. Nancy was a frequent visitor to the city library and managed to read almost every book there on astronomy.

After junior high, Nancy entered the oldest all-girls public school in the United States, Western High School. Her parents encouraged her to take an accelerated course of study, as Nancy had proven herself to be a good student. The school's emphasis on academics is reflected in its motto, *Lucem accepimus, lucem demus*, which means, "We have received light, let us give light."

However, Nancy was not encouraged at the school to become an astronomer. Her guidance counselor questioned Nancy's decision to take a second year of algebra, saying, "What lady would take mathematics—instead of Latin?" Nancy took the math classes she wanted despite the lack of encouragement.

Ask & Answer

Do you think it is important for women to have the same educational opportunities as men? Why or why not?

During her junior year in high school, the Imperial Japanese Navy attacked the United States naval base in Pearl Harbor. This brought the United States into World War II. After Pearl Harbor, many Americans felt that they should be involved in the war effort.

The girls in Nancy's class felt that they should complete their studies sooner so that they could pursue careers or go to college. For this reason, the girls attended classes during the summer to complete their schooling quickly.

 Can you remember an instance during your lifetime when most of the young people in your country felt that it was important to join the same effort?

Women joining the war effort in WW II

"As soon as the sun set, I opened the camera shutter and began collecting starlight . . . . This became a personal quest—me against the star."

—Debra Fischer, American astronomer

OFF TO COLLEGE

Nancy wanted a college with an astronomy program. She chose Swarthmore College outside of Philadelphia, Pennsylvania. Swarthmore had a strong astronomy department that had been started by a woman in 1869. It's founder, Susan Cunningham, had once studied with the famous astronomer Maria Mitchell at Vassar College. Susan devoted her life to Swarthmore. She planned its student observatory, which Nancy would discover during her years at the school.

 Swarthmore had a strong astronomy department that had been started by a woman in 1869.

During her first year at college, Nancy received a solid foundation in astronomy and mathematics. She also studied history and German at her mother's suggestion. Nancy's mother wanted her daughter to take a variety of subjects. But her mother agreed that if astronomy was what Nancy wanted to do, then she would support her.

Cunningham Observatory

Swarthmore's observatory was named after the founder of its astronomy department, Susan Cunningham. The observatory was not used for research, but for instruction. When Nancy first entered the Cunningham Observatory, it was quite neglected. Imagine Nancy's dismay when she discovered that it was being used to store onions!

Still, the observatory contained astronomical tools, including a meridian circle. This was a tool popular in the nineteenth century for tracking the stars as they crossed the meridian. The observatory also contained two telescopes, which Nancy and a classmate took apart and cleaned. Nancy loved the hard work.

By the end of the year, Nancy knew she wanted to major in astronomy. Nancy expressed her interest in science to the dean of women at Swarthmore. Once again, Nancy was not encouraged. The dean was not in favor of any woman pursuing science. She sent Nancy to talk to Peter van de Kamp, chief professor of astronomy.

He made his job seem very dull and didn't paint a very interesting picture of the future for Nancy. But she was determined. Nancy began spending all of her free time in the Cunningham Observatory.

Nancy knew she wanted to major in astronomy, even though she was discouraged by the chief professor of astronomy.

GRADUATE SCHOOL!

Nancy graduated in February 1946 with a degree in astronomy. She received a fellowship for further study. Her father had studied at the University of Chicago and this is where Nancy chose to go to graduate school.

At that time, the astronomy program was housed at the Yerkes Observatory in Wisconsin. Yerkes was well known because many famous scientists, including Edwin Hubble, had worked there. Hubble is the astronomer who discovered that there are many galaxies other than ours. In 1929, he also discovered that the universe is expanding. Hubble's idea that the universe is expanding came to be called the Big Bang theory.

Cool Career: College Professor

Many people working in astronomy are college professors. They teach undergraduate and graduate students about different fields of astronomy. A lot of their time is spent conducting research, testing hypotheses, making discoveries, and writing articles.

As a graduate student, Nancy took courses, worked as a research assistant, and conducted research at the observatory. She often asked her professors for additional work to do during the summers. One of these projects sparked an interest in how stars are classified. She was also interested in the structure of the Milky Way.

 Nancy often asked her professors for additional work during the summers.

In 1949, Nancy completed her PhD. She stayed on at Yerkes, first as an instructor and later as an assistant professor, until 1955.

THE ASSISTANT PROFESSOR

As an assistant professor, Nancy had opportunities to teach graduate courses and to conduct scientific research. Nancy was also able to spend a few months a year at the McDonald Observatory in west Texas.

Ask & Answer

Why do you think astronomers call our galaxy the Milky Way? What characteristics does it have that led to this name?

"The reward of the young scientist is the emotional thrill of being the first person in the history of the world to see something or to understand something."

—Cecilia Payne-Gaposchkin,
American astronomer

The McDonald Observatory is located about 450 miles (724 kilometers) from Austin. At the time, it housed the second-largest telescope in the world.

After reviewing the data she had collected at the McDonald Observatory, Nancy made an exciting discovery. She discovered that stars with different compositions followed different orbits around the galaxy. This was an important clue to how the Milky Way was formed. Her results led to a better understanding of the structure of our galaxy and its history.

 She discovered that stars with different compositions followed different orbits around the galaxy.

As part of Nancy's research into understanding the motion of stars, she looked at the light of stars near the spiral arms of the Milky Way, called the galactic plane. To study a star, astronomers spread its light into a rainbow called a spectrum. The spectrum reveals a lot about a star, from its composition to its speed.

Behind the Discovery

Breaking the light of a star into its colors is called creating a spectrum, which can then be recorded by a special camera. From the spectra, astronomers can know the composition, temperature, and the pressure of the elements in an object. They can also tell whether the object is moving toward or away from us, and at what speed.

While studying stars, Nancy observed a star now known as AG Draconis. Nancy's data said that the star was quite different from the sun, though it had been classified as similar. She wondered if she was observing the right star.

Nancy wrote a brief report on the star and published it in *The Astrophysical Journal*. She never guessed that this star would lead to an exciting invitation in the future.

RADIO ASTRONOMY

Nancy enjoyed teaching at the University of Chicago and Yerkes. But she realized that, as a woman, it was unlikely she would receive a permanent position. When Nancy learned of a job at the U.S. Naval Research Observatory (NRO) in 1955, she took it.

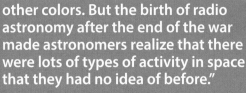

"Up until World War II, we sort of just assumed that stars were bright in the optical—in the part that we could see with our eyes. We didn't pay much attention to the fact that there were other colors. But the birth of radio astronomy after the end of the war made astronomers realize that there were lots of types of activity in space that they had no idea of before."

—Nancy Grace Roman

A year into her work in radio astronomy at NRO in Washington, D.C., Nancy was promoted to the head of the microwave spectroscopy section. But the new position was not all that Nancy had expected it to be. At that time, people were expected to build their own equipment. Nancy did not want to start over as an electronics engineer.

Then she received an unexpected invitation to the opening of an observatory in Armenia. This came because of her work on that strange star, AG Draconis.

Ask & Answer

Why is it sometimes hard to believe new information that goes against old information? Have you ever had to change how you think after learning something new?

Her report had caught the attention of the director of the observatory. Nancy was one of only three American astronomers and the only female invited to the opening.

At this time, Armenia was part of the Soviet Union. Because of an ongoing rivalry between the United States and the Soviet Union known as the Cold War, there were strict restrictions on travel between the two countries.

 Nancy was one of only three American astronomers and the only female invited to the opening.

It wasn't easy for Nancy to obtain permission. But after she took matters into her own hands, including going directly to the Soviet embassy, she was finally successful. When Nancy returned to the United States, she gave a series of popular lectures. People were eager to know about her experiences.

Radio From Outer Space

Radio astronomy had only been discovered in the 1930s. It wasn't until World War II that scientists began investigating radio waves from space. Nancy suspected that radio astronomy would increase our understanding of the universe.

EARLY DAYS OF NASA

Nancy's visit to the Soviet Union caught the attention of NASA. While attending a lecture, Nancy was asked if she knew of someone interested in creating a program at NASA in space astronomy. Nancy thought that she would like the challenge of setting up such a program. She believed the program might influence astronomy for decades.

NASA was only six months old when Nancy joined. It would be a few more years before President John F. Kennedy would announce, in 1961, the United States goal of sending an American safely into space.

Nancy was now NASA's chief astronomer, the first one! Her appointment was big news and she was featured in papers around the country. Though she was praised for being a competent astronomer, the 1950s press was just as likely to mention her hair color as her academic degrees and experience. In one article about her job at NASA, Nancy was pictured cooking! Would a man be pictured this way?

 Nancy was now NASA's chief astronomer, the first one!

What does Nancy's experience with the press tell us about how women in the 1950s were treated differently than they are now?

The 1960s were an exciting time at NASA. Nancy spent 20 years as chief of NASA's Astronomy and Relativity Programs. She worked on incredible projects that measured visible light, x-rays, gamma rays, and radio waves. She studied space with balloons, observatories, and satellites.

The Orbiting Solar Observatory-1 was the first of eight successful NASA astronomical missions. These missions mostly studied the sun using ultraviolet light and x-rays. Nancy was in charge of missions for orbiting astronomical observatories, including *Copernicus*. This observatory was successfully launched into space on August 21, 1972. It made many exciting discoveries, including pulsars.

 Nancy spent 20 years as chief of NASA's Astronomy and Relativity Programs.

Nancy also worked on the Infrared Astronomical Satellite, a joint project between the United States, United Kingdom, and the Netherlands. The space telescope was in operation for only 10 months, but it had a big impact on astronomy.

Astronomers could see the core of the Milky Way for the first time! The space telescope revealed rings of debris around stars. This was an early clue that there were planets beyond our solar system. Could our own solar system have started out that way?

Nancy was a strong supporter of the Hubble Space Telescope. This telescope is an enormous scientific feat. It allows astronomers to make observations of the universe that are not possible from the ground.

The Chilly War

During the 1950s and 1960s, the United States and Russia had a very suspicious, competitive relationship, known as the Cold War. Each country wanted to be the first to send a manmade object into space. When Russia launched *Sputnik* in 1957, and then *Sputnik II* a month later, the United States was astounded! American scientists worked harder than ever to launch a rocket into space. You can learn more about the Space Race during the Cold War at the National Cold War Exhibition at the Royal Air Force Museum in London, England.

Read more about the Space Race at NASA and U.S.-Soviet space cooperation during the Cold War.

Space Race Cold War RAFM London NASA 🔍

Small Astronomical Satellites

While at NASA, Nancy worked on three small astronomical satellites that used x-rays and gamma rays to study the sky, three orbiting solar observatories, and the International Ultraviolet Explorer (IUE). The IUE satellite allowed astronomers to analyze ultraviolet light from the stars in real time. It was the first space observatory to do so. Though designed with a lifespan of only three to five years, the IUE continued to send valuable data to NASA for nearly 19 years. It wasn't shut down until 1996. During those years, the IUE observed more than 100,000 astronomical objects!

From Earth, the atmosphere distorts the view of the sky, making it fuzzy. But the Hubble takes clear pictures from space with no distortion. Then it can send pictures back to Earth from space.

One of Nancy's greatest achievements was bringing together engineers and scientists to determine the tools astronomers needed and how to build them. She convinced her bosses at NASA, who convinced the U.S. Congress that a space telescope was necessary.

Since its launch by NASA in 1990, the Hubble has provided scientists with more than a million observations. And it has revolutionized the study of astronomy.

The Hubble telescope takes pictures and sends them back to Earth from space.

These observations helped scientists determine the approximate age and size of the universe. The Hubble telescope has also enabled the discovery of dark energy, which is a force that is pushing galaxies farther apart.

A HARD-WORKING RETIREMENT

After retiring from NASA, Nancy didn't stop working. She was hired as a consultant to work on NASA's Goddard Space Flight Center. The majority of her work concerned the Hubble Space Telescope.

Nancy was also involved in planning for the Earth Observation System. This system of satellites in the earth's orbit is designed to observe our planet. Later, Nancy worked for the Astronomical Data Center, becoming its director in 1994.

(PS)

The Hubble Space Telescope

You can look at the images taken by the Hubble Space Telescope yourself. What do they make you think of? Can you understand why people might decide to study astronomy after looking at these?

Hubble Space Telescope 🔍

After retiring once again in 1997, Nancy became an active volunteer. She joined Learning Ally, a group that helps dyslexic and learning-disabled people.

Nancy read astronomy books for an organization that produces audiobooks and audio textbooks. She joined Journey to the Universe, a program that places scientists and engineers in schools. She also volunteered with Goddard Space Flight Center's educational outreach program.

AWARDS AND ACHIEVEMENTS

During her long career, Nancy received many honorary degrees and awards. These include the Federal Women's Award for outstanding contributions to government in 1962, and the NASA Exceptional Scientific Achievement Award in 1969. In 1978, she received the NASA Outstanding Scientific Leadership Medal.

Cool Career: Cosmologist

Cosmologists are interested in the origin, evolution, and future of the entire universe. Cosmology overlaps with other sciences, such as physics. Cosmologists often use data gathered by other scientists, who are looking closely at individual aspects of space, to come up with theories about the universe as a whole.

Nancy had several careers as an educator, researcher, and administrator. What does this tell you about how many jobs you may have in the future?

The American Astronomical Society (AAS) recognized Nancy in 1978 with the William Randolf Lovelace II Award. Nancy has even had an asteroid named for her—the Roman 1987!

NASA honored Nancy, in 2011, with a fellowship in her name. She was the first woman to receive this honor and only the fourth person recognized by NASA with a fellowship. The others include Albert Einstein, Edwin Hubble, and Carl Sagan. The Nancy Grace Roman Technology Fellowship is given to recent PhD graduates to help them develop technologies that might lead to scientific breakthroughs.

For almost half of Nancy's career at NASA, she was the highest-ranking female scientist. She succeeded at a time when there were few female scientists and fewer role models. Nancy says now of her choice to pursue astronomy, "I am glad I was stubborn. I have had a wonderful career!"

Ask & Answer

Are awards and recognition important parts of a successful career? Would you be happy to do work you loved if you never received any special thank-you for it?

REACHING OUT

Because she worked hard and achieved so much, Nancy has served as a role model for younger generations of female astronomers. Many magazines, especially publications for women, wanted to feature the first woman to hold an executive position at NASA.

In the 1960s, Nancy was the most visible role model for women who were interested in pursuing a career in space. In her role as a mentor for young women, Nancy often stressed the fact that her job was demanding. However, she was quick to add that, if space science was what really interested you, it could be a very rewarding career.

Long after retiring from NASA, Nancy continued to be an inspiration. She always shared her passion for science. As a volunteer, Nancy taught astronomy to all ages and gave presentations around the country.

ASTRONOMY TEAM

In 1979, the American Astronomical Society (AAS) created the Committee on the Status of Women in Astronomy (CSWA). The CSWA makes recommendations to the AAS Council to improve the status of women in astronomy and to encourage more women into the astronomy field. The committee publishes a newsletter, a magazine, and a blog. You can read more about it. Why do you think there is a special committee for women in astronomy? Do you think men need a committee, too? Why or why not?

CWSA newsletter blog magazine 🔍

Now, at 90 years old, Nancy participates in discussions on the role of women in science through videos. In 2010, Women in Aerospace recognized Nancy with an achievement award for both her work on the Hubble Space Telescope and for her pioneering career in astronomy.

"My career was quite unusual, so my main advice to someone interested in a career similar to my own is to remain open to change and new opportunities...."

—Nancy Grace Roman

Chapter 3

MAGGIE ADERIN-POCOCK

The definition of a curve ball is "something that is unexpected or surprising." It is also a word that Margaret Ebunoluwa Aderin-Pocock, or Maggie, uses to describe her life. Maggie was born in London, on March 9, 1968. She decided as a young child that she wanted to be a space scientist.

The 1960s was an exciting time in the history of spaceflight. The year Maggie was born, 1968, NASA launched *Apollo 8*. It was the first mission to take humans to the moon and back. Tens of thousands of people gathered at Cape Canaveral, Florida, to watch the launch. The mission was an outstanding success. *Apollo 8* flew twice around the moon, proving that the moon was reachable.

 The year Maggie was born, 1968, NASA launched *Apollo 8*.

The following year, *Apollo 11* became the first mission to land astronauts on the moon. Around the world, images of Neil Armstrong and Buzz Aldrin walking on the boulder-strewn lunar surface held people spellbound. Space exploration was thrilling!

Ask & Answer

Has an event that happened in your lifetime sparked the same kind of excitement as the moon landing in 1969?

One Small Step

Landing on the moon was a major accomplishment. You can watch the landing and listen to the voices of the people involved in the mission. What do you think it was like for people on Earth to watch this?

moon landing *Apollo 11* 🔍

For Maggie, these events planted a dream in her mind that she never forgot. Her work on satellites and telescopes and as a science communicator has increased people's knowledge of space. It has made people think about how they, too, can be a part of this exciting science.

FAMILY LIFE

Maggie's parents moved to England from Nigeria in the 1950s for a better life. While her father had dreams of studying medicine in the United Kingdom, these dreams were never realized.

Instead, he held a variety of jobs to support the family. He managed a Pizza Express restaurant and ran his own importing and exporting business. Maggie's mother worked as a counselor and later, briefly, as a co-host on a talk show called *House Party*.

There were four girls in the Aderin family. Maggie was the third. When Maggie was four years old her parents divorced, and the girls were split up into pairs between the parents. Maggie and her youngest sister were kept together while her older sisters stayed with a different parent.

During the next 14 years, Maggie moved 13 times! Maggie has said it was a difficult time, but her mother taught her how to be adaptable and advised her to make the best of any situation. And that is exactly what Maggie did. She learned to talk to new people and make friends easily.

Ask & Answer

How does your childhood affect the kind of person you are as a teenager? As an adult?

EARLY INFLUENCES

As a young child, Maggie loved watching science-fiction television shows. She especially liked the BBC children's program *The Clangers*. The animation was very simple but the plots were full of entertaining story lines. The series began airing only four months after the NASA moon landing. *The Clangers* actually staged a comeback in 2015.

The Clangers

The Clangers is a show about small, mouse-like creatures who live on a small planet. They speak in whistles and eat blue string soup! You can watch clips of old episodes. Do you think these would be popular today? Why or why not?

The Clangers blue string soup 🔍

Maggie enjoyed watching the adventures of the pink, mouse-like Clangers on their rocky, moon-like planet. Would they fish for gold coins among the stars? Where would their musical fishing boats take them next? A stuffed Clanger often accompanies Maggie when she gives talks today.

When Maggie was a little older, shows such as *Star Trek* appealed to her. She especially liked the cast of characters from different cultures on the spaceship *Enterprise* and how they worked together.

 As a young child, Maggie loved watching science-fiction television shows.

Maggie's favorite character on *Star Trek* was Spock, who was always in turmoil because he was part human, part Vulcan. Like Spock, Maggie felt pulled between two worlds because she was a child of Nigerian immigrants living in London.

What television programs or books have inspired you and why?

As Maggie had never been to Nigeria, she didn't feel that she was a "real" Nigerian. At school, children told her that she wasn't British because her skin was darker.

She often felt isolated. Out of this isolation came a love for space, which Maggie saw as a place that welcomed everyone. "If you look at the earth from space, you don't see the divisions," she says in an interview with the BBC. "Space almost unifies the earth, because when you look at it remotely, you get the feeling that we're one. Down here it often doesn't feel that way."

OFF TO SCHOOL

Initially, Maggie found school very difficult. Around the age of five, she had to repeat a year. At the age of six, Maggie was diagnosed with dyslexia. Dyslexia happens when the brain does not recognize symbols. Letters may appear backward, upside down, or mixed up. Because of this disability, reading and writing did not come easily to Maggie. She didn't just dislike reading—she hated it!

Maggie was put in special classes for struggling students where expectations for her were very low. Maggie has said that she was "expected to do little more than play with safety scissors and glitter."

 Because of dyslexia, reading and writing did not come easily to Maggie.

Even though Maggie knew that her teachers didn't have high expectations for her, she had them for herself. One day, in the school library, a book caught Maggie's eye. It showed an astronaut floating in space. She thought the book was beautiful. She also realized that she wanted to go to space.

DISCOVERING SCIENCE

Another day, while still in public school, Maggie made a startling discovery about herself. Her math teacher asked the class a simple question: "If you have a liter of water and that liter of water contains 1,000 cubic milliliters, then how much does one cubic centimeter of water weigh?"

She Says

"The human brain is greater yet, because it can comprehend it all."

—Antonia Maury, American astronomer

Maggie was sure of the answer—1 gram. She quickly raised her hand. She felt proud that she knew the answer. For the first time, Maggie had something at school she was good at. Suddenly, science was appealing. Maggie realized that studying science was the way to space.

When Maggie revealed her wish to become a space scientist, her teachers weren't supportive. They suggested that she consider nursing because she had a caring personality. But Maggie didn't follow that well-intentioned advice. She had other ideas.

 Maggie realized that studying science was the way to space.

Maggie turned something in her life that was hard—moving all the time—into an important part of her success. Each time Maggie changed schools, she turned the move into an opportunity to join advanced classes. New teachers were unaware of her dyslexia, so they did not stereotype her. They didn't assume that she couldn't do hard schoolwork. Maggie learned that new teachers were more likely to support her dreams.

AN EYE ON SPACE

With her newfound passion for science, Maggie began to read more, not just at school but at home. As her reading improved, so did her grades.

Cool Career: Space Educator

Have you ever visited a planetarium? Space educators give presentations, classes, and lectures to the public to share their knowledge and interest in astronomy. They are an important link to the next generation of astronomers!

Before long, Maggie was at the top of her class. She found a strong supporter in her father. He believed that education was very important and wanted Maggie to succeed.

What Maggie really wanted was a telescope to study the sky. She was a fan of astronomer Carl Sagan's show, *Cosmos*, which took her on a journey through space from her own living room. Now, *Cosmos* is hosted by the very popular cosmologist Neil deGrasse Tyson.

She bought a simple telescope with her own money. Eagerly, Maggie held the telescope up to the sky. What wondrous moon landscape would it reveal? Sadly, the telescope was not a very good one. All Maggie saw was a blur of color. It was definitely not the dramatic view of the sky she had hoped for.

One day, Maggie saw an advertisement for a class on making telescopes. Maybe this was the solution! She enrolled and soon she was making her own telescopes.

Part of the process involved placing coarse powder between two pieces of glass and rubbing for many hours. After six months, Maggie was finally able to go outside and hold her new telescope up to the moon.

The moment was magical. She could see the craters on the moon and the rings of Saturn! After making her first telescope, Maggie wanted to make more space instruments.

JOCELYN BELL BURNELL

Susan "Jocelyn" Bell Burnell, born in 1943, was introduced to astronomy by her father. He was an architect who also wrote books. His books on astronomy interested Jocelyn. Later, in high school, Jocelyn was fortunate to have a dedicated physics teacher. He allowed Jocelyn to work in the lab after school. She then decided to study physics at the University of Glasgow. From there, she went to the University of Cambridge to work on her doctorate in radio astronomy.

In 1967, Jocelyn used a large radio telescope designed by Antony Hewish (her advisor at Cambridge) and Martin Ryle to investigate signals coming from collapsed stars. The media called these pulsars. Her male colleagues received the Nobel Prize for their work.

PURSUING HER DREAM

Though Maggie's father wanted her to study medicine and her mother suggested that she become an actress, Maggie had other ideas. In her final years of high school, Maggie took physics, chemistry, biology, and math. She found biology interesting, but she decided to pursue physics. Physics interested Maggie because she felt it was the study of everything.

Many people felt that Bell deserved to win as well but she said, "Nobel Prizes are based on longstanding research, not on a flash-in-the-pan observation of a research student. The award to me would have debased the prize." But Bell did receive other awards for that work. These came from the American Astronomical Society and the Royal Astronomical Society. She shared the Franklin Institute's Michelson Medal with Hewish.

Since the discovery, Bell has held many executive and teaching positions in the United Kingdom. She is currently the visiting professor of astrophysics at Oxford.

Watch an interview with Jocelyn in which she discusses her discoveries.

"Jocelyn Bell Burnell" discoveries 🔍

Maggie felt that physics would allow her to get closer to the stars. It would give her an understanding of the universe.

Maggie was accepted into London's prestigious Imperial College. Founded in 1907, Imperial is one of the top-ranked colleges in the world. From 1987 until 1990, Maggie studied physics. During the last year of her degree, she began specializing in optics.

After finishing her undergraduate degree, Maggie pursued her PhD. She wanted to study physics, but didn't find a program that felt exactly right.

Ask & Answer

Maggie turned her disappointment at her first telescope into a career. Have you ever been disappointed by the quality of something you saved up for? What did you do?

When an optical project came up in the mechanical engineering department at Imperial College, Maggie decided to pursue it for her thesis. She was a determined and enthusiastic student. From 1990 to 1994, Maggie worked on a project developing optics for measuring engine oils more efficiently. The system she created is still being used today.

THE WORKING WORLD

After graduation, Maggie worked for the British Ministry of Defense on a missile warning system. Later, she designed handheld land mine detectors.

She loved the job because she was working on a project that had the potential to save lives. Through this experience, she was able to visit Cambodia and meet the young victims of land mines.

Even though she loved her job, she never forgot her dream of being a space scientist. In 1999, she made the move into space science by making a spectrograph for the Gemini telescope in Chile. A spectrograph splits the light from an astronomical object into its rainbow of colors, which astronomers use to discover what the object is made of and how it moves in space.

Gemini Telescopes

There are actually two Gemini telescopes, one in Chile and one in Hawaii. These regions have dry climates and little light pollution. The Gemini telescopes are used by scientists all around the world, and are operated by a partnership made of six countries, including the United States and Britain. You can learn more about the telescopes and see pictures of the phenomena that have been observed with them.

Gemini telescope pictures

With a fellowship from the Science and Technology Facilities Council, Maggie joined a group at the University College London. For two years, she worked on the high-resolution spectrograph for the Gemini telescope in Chile. The telescope's mirror is a massive 8 meters (26 feet) in diameter!

Maggie found this experience to be one of the highlights of her career. She packed the spectrograph into 28 boxes and traveled to Chile, where she re-assembled the spectrograph by herself.

Maggie loved being in the Southern Hemisphere because she could gaze directly into the center of the Milky Way. She was having such a good time that after six months her family wondered if she was ever going to come home!

 Maggie found her experience with the spectrograph to be one of the highlights of her career.

When she finally returned to Britain in 2004, she received a job offer from Astrium, the third-largest aerospace company in the world. Instead of working on ground-based space instruments, Maggie would be designing ones made for space.

Maggie began working on numerous projects, including European Space Agency satellites. In one project, Maggie's team created a satellite system for monitoring the earth's atmosphere.

The Next Hubble

While at Astrium, Maggie was part of a team working on one of the instruments for the James Webb Space Telescope. It is called the NIRSpec, short for Near Infrared Spectrograph.

The James Webb is run by NASA with help from the European Space Agency and the Canadian Space Agency. It will continue and go beyond the great work of the Hubble Space Telescope. Four science instruments will enable the telescope to detect light from stars, galaxies, and planets that orbit other stars. It will even be able to detect light from 13.5 billion years ago!

Some of the objects the James Webb will study are extremely faint. So the telescope will have to look at them for hundreds of hours to collect enough light to form a spectrum.

You can learn more about the James Webb Telescope below.

If you would like to see the difference between this telescope and a common telescope you might find in a store, NASA has a great online game for you.

James Webb telescope NIRSpec vs common telescope 🔍

In Her Own Words

Maggie has been surprised at how well her degrees in physics and mechanical engineering have combined for her work making satellites. You can hear her talk about her career here.

"Maggie Aderin-Pocock" satellites 🔍

Maggie worked on the satellite *Aeolus*, named after a Greek mythical character who ruled the winds. This satellite measures wind speeds across the earth and helps scientists with weather predictions.

Blue Peter was a satellite project sponsored by the Natural Environment Research Council and BBC. As part of the International Year of Astronomy in 2009, the *Blue Peter*, a British children's television program, wanted to launch its own satellite to interest children in space. Maggie was an important part of this project. Children were able to see the satellite being made and launched. Plus, it sent back images to Earth!

Ask & Answer

Is education for kids only? Why is it important for adults to learn new things?

THE SCIENCE COMMUNICATOR

Building instruments was a lot of fun, but Maggie was also interested in sharing her love of science with children. In her work she was noticing that it was difficult to find people to hire who had the necessary science skills. Maggie decided to encourage young people to study science. These were the future scientists.

In 2004, with her husband, Dr. Martin Pocock, Maggie started a company called Science Innovation Ltd. One of the company's projects, a 3-D computer program called *Celestia*, leads children on imaginary tours of the universe. Since beginning her company, Maggie has given talks to more than 120,000 people around the world. More than half of those have been children in the United Kingdom.

 Maggie was also interested in sharing her love of science with children.

One of the most popular questions she is asked about is life on other planets. Maggie says that she believes intelligent life is out there. Why? Because our galaxy has a few hundred billion stars, most of which have planets. And our galaxy is only one of a few hundred billion galaxies in the universe!

In addition to school presentations, Maggie's company produced a documentary called *Space in the UK*. The series was split into six episodes and featured Maggie aboard an imaginary spaceship. Initially distributed through schools and science fairs in the United Kingdom, it's now available on iTunes.

Maggie was still working for Astrium during this time. In 2006, she was awarded a Science in Society fellowship from the U.K.'s Science and Technology Facilities Council.

The fellowship allows scientists to spend more time in the community promoting the sciences. With this fellowship, Maggie could consider becoming more involved in science education.

Space in the UK

You can listen to *Space in the UK* on iTunes for free.

"Space in the UK" iTunes 🔍

Take a Tour

Maggie's bubbly personality has made her computer program, *Celestia*, very popular. It engages children and holds their interest by making science understandable and fun. You can check it out yourself.

Celestia computer program 🔍

A MEDIA STAR IS BORN

Although Maggie had no formal training in broadcast journalism, she was a natural in front of the camera. Her engaging style and her skill at explaining science and scientific tools won over many new fans.

She was the planetary scientist in a six-part BBC documentary, *The Cosmos: A Beginner's Guide.* Maggie displayed her expertise on a range of topics, from telescopes to explaining the mysteries of space.

"Fame is fleeting. My numbers mean more to me than my name. If astronomers are still using my data years from now, that's my greatest compliment."

—Vera Rubin, American astronomer

In one segment of *The Cosmos*, Maggie went to Pisa, Italy, to see a massive telescope used to look for gravity waves. The *Virgo's* two arms each measure 1.8 miles (nearly 3 kilometers) long.

Another early media job was as the scientific consultant for the series *Paradox*, a science-fiction police drama. She also appeared on the BBC documentary series, *Doctor Who Confidential*. This was a look behind the scenes of the famous science-fiction show, *Doctor Who*.

Ask & Answer

How might science fiction inspire people to study science?

In March 2010, she appeared on the BBC Radio 4 program, *Desert Island Discs*. In this biographical radio program, each guest chooses the music, book, and luxury item they would take to a desert island. Maggie's musical choice was *As* by Stevie Wonder and her book choice was *Star Maker* by Olaf Stapledon. Her luxury item, not surprisingly, was a telescope.

  Although Maggie had no formal training in broadcast journalism, she was a natural in front of the camera.

On the News

Maggie began appearing to explain scientific phenomenon on television and news programs, such as *Newsnight* with Jeremy Paxman. She always tries to create excitement about science and understanding of its principles through models and demonstrations. You can watch Maggie in action as she explains why the moon looks blood red during a lunar eclipse.

blood moon *Newsnight* "Maggie Aderin-Pocock" 🔍

Shortly after the birth of her daughter, Laurie, in 2010, Maggie received an exciting email from the BBC asking her to make a documentary. Maggie said, "Yes!" She and her family traveled around the world to make the documentary, *Do We Really Need the Moon?* In it she explores the importance of the moon and its gravity on our tides. *Do We Really Need the Moon?* earned Maggie the Talkback Thames New Talent Award.

This documentary was followed in 2012 by a second documentary series on BBC Two about why we need satellites. For her role in the documentary, *In Orbit: How Satellites Rule Our World*, Maggie drew on her years of experience building satellites. She explained to her eager viewers all about the technology of satellites and how they are transforming lives.

Cool Career: Engineer

When astronauts travel to space, they want to know that skilled engineers designed their spacecraft! Aerospace engineers have to build carriers and equipment to withstand conditions that are out of this world. They need to expect the unexpected while they solve problems before they happen. The machines that support life in space are all designed by qualified aerospace engineers.

In 2014, Maggie became a presenter on the BBC's longest running astronomy series, *The Sky at Night*. Now, Maggie works with astrophysicist Chris Lintott, who founded Zooniverse, and solar researcher Lucie Green to explain astronomy and space-related subjects to a wide audience.

For Maggie, appearing on the show is the fulfillment of a lifelong dream. When she was a small child, Maggie begged her parents to let her stay up late to watch the program. Little did she realize that one day she would be a host!

RECOGNITION

Since embarking on a career as a space scientist, Maggie has received numerous honors. In 2009, Staffordshire University presented Maggie with an honorary degree for her contributions to the field of science education.

The following year, the British Science Association awarded Maggie an honorary fellowship. She has also earned three Science in Society fellowships from the Science and Technology Facilities Council in 2006, 2008, and 2010.

In 2009, Maggie was awarded a prestigious Member of the Order of the British Empire. This was for her outstanding contributions in science and education. The honor is given by the queen of England.

Besides her career as a space scientist and a science communicator, Maggie enjoys spending time with her daughter. She also likes watching movies and going for walks in the countryside. Encouraging young people around the world has become an important mission.

Though Maggie has achieved much, she still has space dreams. Someday, Maggie would like to fly to Mars. And who knows, maybe the passengers on that ship will be the students she has inspired to follow their dreams into space.

"You don't need a brain the size of a small planet to understand, participate in, and enjoy science."

—Maggie Aderin-Pocock

Chapter 4

ANDREA GHEZ

Andrea Ghez is an astronomer and physicist. She is also a detective. Unlike Sherlock Holmes, though, she does not wander foggy cobblestone streets lit by gaslight. She does not have a sidekick named Watson or a pipe. Andrea uses different tools and sophisticated techniques to reveal secrets hiding in the Milky Way. She is working to solve the mystery of how the universe was formed!

For more than 15 years, Andrea has worked with the world's two largest telescopes. These are built on the summit of Mauna Kea, a dormant volcano in Hawaii.

The large mirrors of the Keck telescopes at the W.M. Keck Observatory measure the width of a tennis court. Their massive eyes are so powerful that they can capture starlight from distant galaxies. They allow astronomers, including Andrea, to look billions of years into the past.

Andrea does not use the telescopes to solve a crime. She has used them to unravel one of the biggest mysteries of this century: What is in the middle of the Milky Way?

Ask & Answer

Can you think of other mysteries that exist in nature? Why do we find mysteries so fascinating?

In the 1700s, mathematician Pierre-Simon Laplace and philosopher John Michell thought there were dense objects in the middle of the Milky Way. What if these objects had a gravitational pull so strong that not even light could escape?

Albert Einstein referred to this in his theory of general relativity in 1915. In 1967, a physicist named John Wheeler called this fascinating object a black hole.

Black Holes

A black hole is a place in space where gravity is so strong that nothing can escape, not even light. We can't see black holes, but we know they're there because of the way stars and other astronomical bodies behave around them.

Black holes are caused when the center of a massive star collapses in on itself and becomes very dense. You can see illustrations of what a black hole might look like.

black holes collapsing stars 🔍

Scientists discussed the possibility of a black hole lurking in the center of our galaxy. But they had no proof. That is until Andrea and her research team, the Galactic Center Group at UCLA, took the case.

Andrea used her skills as an astronomer plus new, powerful technology. That's how she saw through the clouds of dust and gas surrounding the heart of the Milky Way. Andrea and her team proved that, yes, there is a massive black hole in our galaxy. The discovery of a black hole in the middle of the Milky Way amazed scientists and captured the public's curiosity.

 Andrea used telescopes to unravel one of the biggest mysteries of this century: What is in the middle of the Milky Way?

Cool Career: Planetologist

Planetologists study planets! They do experiments and make observations to find out what planets are made of, how they were created, and what their relationship is to other celestial bodies. They pay attention to the geology of planets and to whether or not a planet has an atmosphere. And planetologists don't just study other planets. They also study Earth!

CHILDHOOD

Andrea Mia Ghez was born on June 16, 1965, in New York, New York. She was the first of three children of Susanne and Gilbert Ghez. Andrea's mother was the former curator at the Renaissance Society, an art museum in Chicago. Her father is a professor of management and economics at Roosevelt University in Chicago.

Andrea spent the first few years of her life in New York City. There was a lot to explore along its busy streets, including Central Park. Soon, the family grew to include Andrea's younger sister, Mimi. Later, the Ghezes moved to Chicago, Illinois, where Andrea's youngest sister, Helena, was born.

Like many young children, Andrea filled her days with a variety of hobbies. She was involved in dance and loved challenging herself with all sorts of puzzles, from jigsaws to brainteasers.

She had a brief interest in space, but Andrea never seriously thought about becoming a professional astronomer until much later.

Andrea's childhood coincided with a dynamic time in the history of space exploration. Three years before Andrea was born, President John F. Kennedy delivered his now-famous speech in which he challenged the United States to reach the moon. Before Andrea even got to kindergarten, she was caught up in the excitement of NASA's Apollo missions.

 Andrea's childhood coincided with a dynamic time in the history of space exploration.

President Kennedy's Challenge

In his September 12, 1962, speech, President Kennedy set the goal of going to the moon. He said, "Many years ago the great British explorer George Mallory, who was to die on Mount Everest, was asked why did he want to climb it. He said, 'Because it is there.' Well, space is there, and we're going to climb it, and the moon and the planets are there, and new hopes for knowledge and peace are there."

Can you remember what you wanted to be when you were younger? If so, has your choice of career changed or stayed the same and why do you think this is?

During this decade, the whole world was buzzing with news of NASA's Apollo program. "Reaching into Unexplored Frontiers" and "Zooming Toward Moon" were some of the news headlines of the decade. They reflected the public's excitement about the space program. This was a great time to be a child interested in space exploration.

The Apollo program lasted from 1967 to 1972. It involved 12 manned missions into space. The most famous mission was *Apollo 11*. On July 20, 1969, Neil Armstrong and "Buzz" Aldrin met the president's goal when they landed on the moon and explored the lunar surface. About 600 million people worldwide, including the Ghez family, watched the moon landing.

The event inspired four-year-old Andrea to make an announcement to her family. She told them that she was going to be the first woman on the moon.

This was a great time to be a child interested in space exploration.

Women In Space Program

During the 1960s, a few elite female aviators took part in a privately funded program that tested their astronaut skills. Women in Space candidates performed a rigorous series of tests. These included being spun around and around in a simulator that replicated the tumbling effects of space. Ice water was spurted into their ears to bring on vertigo. They endured sitting in an isolation tank for hours.

Of the 19 women who took part in the tests, 13 successfully completed them all. The problem was that NASA required all astronauts to be military jet test pilots in 1962. Unfortunately, this was not a career open to women. So even though the 13 women proved they had the skills to be an astronaut, American women could not become astronauts. The program was shut down.

The first female astronaut was Russian. In 1963, Valentina Tereshkova made history when she flew into space. It was another 20 years before the United States sent a woman into space—Sally Ride in 1983. You can read more about the Women in Space Program and watch interviews with women astronomers.

Women in Space Program PBS 🔍

Andrea's parents wanted to encourage their daughter's excitement about space. So they bought her a telescope. Once her home was transformed into an observatory, Andrea used the telescope to gaze up at Earth's nearest neighbor, the moon.

But her early enthusiasm for space ended when other entertainments got in the way. There were so many things to do besides crater hop on the moon! It would be more than a decade before Andrea revisited her space dreams.

SCHOOL DAYS

Andrea and her sisters attended the University of Chicago Lab Schools. Thriving at the school, which was known for its flexible, educational approach, she especially enjoyed working on independent projects. Andrea was an intelligent and curious student who approached each new topic as if it were a puzzle.

During her investigations, Andrea looked at each problem from different angles. She always wanted to know how and why things worked.

There were many afterschool activities to choose from. Andrea had a passion for ballet and later expressed an interest in choreography.

Choreography is like a puzzle—the individual steps are the pieces that fit together to create a dance. But by the time Andrea entered high school, she realized how hard a ballerina's life could be. Mathematics had become her new interest and she was excellent at it. After learning of a study claiming boys were better at math, Andrea challenged her male classmates.

Dancing with the Stars

Andrea's interest moved from dancing to mathematics and astronomy, but perhaps those subjects aren't as different as you might think. They both involve problem solving and hard work. The University of California, Los Angeles, used home movies of Andrea dancing for its 2014 Centennial campaign. You can watch the video. Do you find it inspiring?

UCLA 2014 Centennial campaign "Andrea Ghez" 🔍

An outgoing student, Andrea was involved in several clubs. She was a member of the school's field hockey and track teams. She enjoyed music and photography. She liked reading mysteries and was excellent at solving puzzles, too.

Andrea also had fun thinking about questions—really big questions! She wanted to know how the universe worked.

Andrea was an intelligent and curious student who approached each new topic as if it were a puzzle.

IMPORTANT INFLUENCES

Andrea was always a curious person. She enjoyed investigating, imagining, and questioning the world around her. Sometimes, Andrea's dad made up math problems for her to solve just for the fun of it. Andrea's many interests—from sports to dance to music—were encouraged at school and at home. Her parents had high expectations and hopes for her future. Do you think these expectations had an affect on her? Are high expectations good or bad?

Andrea's mother, Susanne, was her earliest role model. Susanne demonstrated the importance of balancing a career with family responsibilities.

Ask & Answer

Andrea encountered only one female science teacher during high school. How does this compare to your school? Would having more female science teachers in elementary and middle schools encourage more girls to study science?

Earhart Crater

Amelia Earhart is well known as the first woman to fly alone across the Atlantic Ocean. But did you know there's also a crater on the moon named after her? In 2015, researchers at Purdue University discovered a 124-mile-wide buried crater on the side of the moon that faces Earth. Amelia was a part of the faculty at Purdue's Department of Aeronautics from 1935 until her disappearance in 1938, when her plane is believed to have crashed in the Pacific Ocean. Craters are traditionally named after scientists or explorers, and Amelia certainly fits the role.

Andrea was encouraged to believe that she could do great things. She was also taught that in order to achieve her goals, she would have to work hard.

Andrea found role models in books and was drawn to real stories of female explorers. She especially enjoyed reading about the historic career of Amelia Earhart, who was one of the few female pilots in the 1920s. Amelia's life inspired many young women to be adventurous and determined.

In high school, Andrea was influenced by her math and science teachers. She credits Ms. Keene, her chemistry teacher, for inspiring her to pursue science.

Cool Career: Astronaut

When many people think of jobs in astronomy, they think of astronauts. Traveling to space is the ultimate business trip! Astronauts train for many years to learn to fly, survive in extreme conditions, such as zero gravity, and perform research and experiments in space. As of 2014, only 536 people had ever traveled to space.

Ms. Keene was Andrea's only female science teacher during high school. But her presence encouraged Andrea to believe that women belong in science.

COLLEGE YEARS

After graduating from high school, Andrea was accepted into Massachusetts Institute of Technology (MIT) in Boston. Andrea saw herself pursuing a PhD from the moment she entered college. She wanted to achieve the highest level of education possible. Education, Andrea felt, would qualify her for any job she chose.

Andrea would later refer to her schooling as "a coat of armor" in a 2014 interview with the National Science Foundation. What do you think she meant by this? How does education protect people?

> Andrea want to achieve the highest level of education possible. Education, she felt, would qualify her for any job she chose.

Andrea entered MIT planning to major in math. However, the college offered so many courses of study that Andrea found it difficult to decide. She had a real talent for science and was interested in everything from chemistry to aerospace engineering.

Finally, Andrea chose physics. She made this choice because it allowed her to ask many of those big questions that had long held her fascination. "In college," says Andrea in an interview with *StarDate Online*, "I think I changed my major almost as often as I changed my socks."

HOOKED ON ASTRONOMY

Remember the little girl who asked her parents for a telescope after watching the first moon landing? Andrea rediscovered that passion for space during her third year of college.

Through a physics teacher, Andrea was given the opportunity to conduct research at the Kitt Peak National Observatory in the Quinlan Mountains of the Arizona-Sonoran Desert. Andrea threw herself into the experience. She took on every task, from opening the dome to taking pictures of the night sky.

P. Marenfeld & NOAO/AURA/NSF

By the end of her adventure at the Kitt Peak National Observatory in Arizona, Andrea knew that astronomy would be her life's work. It was exciting! In 2013, Andrea told Nature.com that she "fell in love with the whole profession."

ANNIE JUMP CANNON

Annie Jump Cannon was born December 11, 1863, in Dover, Delaware. From a young age, Annie was interested in astronomy. She regularly observed the stars and taught herself to recognize the constellations.

Annie went to Wellesley College to study physics and graduated in 1884. Several years later, Annie returned to Wellesley as a student of astronomy. While working at Harvard College Observatory classifying stars, Annie devised a classification for the stars based on their temperatures.

In 1987, Andrea graduated from MIT with a bachelor of science degree in physics. Andrea decided to study astronomy and astrophysics at a graduate program at California Technical Institute (Caltech) in Pasadena, which owns the Palomar Observatory in San Diego County.

NEWBORN STARS

Andrea had been wondering what to study in graduate school for quite some time. Just as in her earlier years, she still thought about big problems. Andrea wanted to study black holes.

Another woman working at the observatory, Henrietta Swan Leavitt, saw that the stars in each category were similar in color. The system is now known as the Harvard spectral classification scheme.

Over her years at the observatory, Annie classified 400,000 stars! During her 40-year career she became the first woman to be honored with the Henry Draper Medal from the U.S. National Academy of Sciences. Later, she received the Ellen Richards Research Prize and used the money to set up her own award. Today, the Annie Jump Cannon Award is given each year to a woman of distinction in the field of astronomy.

She joined a group at Caltech working on increasing the resolution of a speckle imager. This device takes thousands of photos and combines them into one crisp image. Andrea's group hoped to use it to see the centers of galaxies.

However, Andrea met a setback. The technology was not yet advanced enough to produce the image quality she needed for this study. So Andrea changed the focus of her research to studying the births of young stars. She wanted to know if stars usually had companions or if they were born alone.

 Just as in her earlier years, she still thought about big problems.

Andrea tackled the problem with infrared detectors. These are able to pick up on the heat signatures released by stars at the beginning of their lives. She also modified the speckle imaging technique that produces high-resolution images.

To conduct her research, Andrea used large telescopes around the world, including the 200-inch Hale Telescope at the Palomar Observatory. At the time, it was the largest telescope on Earth.

The work was challenging. But Andrea's two Caltech mentors were there to offer their support. These were Keith Matthews, chief instrument scientist of the infrared astronomy group, and astrophysicist Gerry Neugebauer.

One Star or Two?

Scientists have long known that stars are born in turbulent clouds of gas and dust. What they didn't know before Andrea completed her research was why the majority of stars in the Milky Way have one or more companions. Binary stars are two stars that orbit each other. There are also multiple star systems. Our sun is a single star. Researchers wanted to know if it was unusual for stars to be born as singles.

The results of Andrea's study, completed in 1992, were exciting. Her research showed that most stars begin their lives with a companion. Andrea explained in a 2006 *Nova* interview, "The most likely kind of system that's going to host an Earth-like planet is a star that doesn't have a companion. And that is not the norm."

 Andrea's research showed that most stars begin their lives with a companion.

Scientists now believe that stars form in clusters. Some stars drift away or are ejected from their cluster and that's what happened to our sun.

Andrea received her PhD from Caltech in 1993, then was chosen for a prestigious Hubble Postdoctoral Fellowship. This is awarded to scientists whose research is related to current or future NASA missions.

A Star Is Born

Just as living things have life cycles, stars go through several phases during their lifetimes. You can learn more about the life cycle of a star from NASA.

star's life cycle NASA   🔍

After working as a researcher at the University of Arizona's Steward Observatory, Andrea joined the faculty of UCLA as a professor of astronomy and physics.

HUNTING FOR A BLACK HOLE

It was a perfect time for her to go to the University of California. The massive new W.M. Keck Observatory had just opened. This observatory is jointly operated by Caltech and the University of California.

The telescope's mirrors are a whopping 33 feet in diameter. Nine of the mirrors lined up would be as long as a football field! The mirrors are made of 36 hexagonal segments, like the eyes of insects. A hexagon is a shape with six sides.

Andrea planned to use the telescopes with the speckle imaging technique that she had so successfully used in graduate school. But the first time she proposed this study, Andrea was turned down. Andrea's colleagues felt that her technique wouldn't work. But she didn't give up.

Andrea gave many talks on the subject. Finally, she convinced the people she worked with that her ideas on how to use the telescope were good ones.

Andrea focused her research on the center of the Milky Way. This was where scientists had long suspected that there was a black hole. In 1931, Karl Jansky discovered powerful radio waves coming from this area. Researchers thought that these waves could be coming from a jet of particles streaming away from the black hole.

At first, Andrea's colleagues felt that her technique wouldn't work. But she didn't give up.

Andrea and her team faced the daunting task of proving a black hole existed. How do you prove something that's invisible? Andrea knew that black holes have huge amounts of mass in small spaces. The gravitational pull from this mass would be very strong. In fact, it would be so strong that nearby stars would orbit the mass extraordinarily fast.

Ask & Answer

Andrea learned about black holes by observing things around them. Are there other things in nature that we can't see and have to study in this way?

"Do not look at stars as bright spots only. Try to take in the vastness of the universe."

—Maria Mitchell, early astronomer

Andrea began tracking the movement of 200 stars close to the center of the galaxy. It wasn't an easy task. For one thing, the center of the universe is like the downtown of a city. The closer you are to the center of the Milky Way, the more traffic there is. There are thousands of stars swirling around!

Andrea also had to deal with the earth's atmosphere. Air currents in the atmosphere make the starlight that travels 26,000 years from the center of the Milky Way dance and twinkle.

 Andrea began tracking the movement of 200 stars close to the center of the galaxy. It wasn't an easy task.

Andrea had continued to refine the technique of speckle imaging. Her team used her speckle imaging technique on the Keck telescope in Hawaii to produce sharper images. The process requires thousands of snapshots to be taken and stitched together using a computer.

The team had a huge breakthrough with a new technique called adaptive optics. How does it work?

An orange laser beam is shot from the Keck telescope, 60 miles into the sky. The laser is aimed right next to the star astronomers want to study.

The laser beam creates a disc-shaped image that looks like an artificial star. Meanwhile, a computer back on Earth analyzes the information and adjusts the Keck's mirror up to 2,000 times a second to reshape the light into a sharp image similar to what you'd see from a space telescope.

WORKING AT THE W.M. KECK OBSERVATORY

At the time, Andrea had access to the Keck telescope only a few nights each year. She had to share it with many scientists from around the world! When they were there, the team slept all day, got up mid-afternoon, and drove to the summit. If the night was cloudy, though, there would be no views of the stars.

In an interview, Andrea said, "(Sometimes) you'll feel like a project is cursed if you have only one night, and that night is lost. There's too much to do in too little time."

In 1995, Andrea's group was able to get a clear photo of the galaxy's center. They recorded the measurements and then the process of tracking the orbits of 200 stars began!

 Andrea had to share the Keck telescope with many scientists from around the world!

The Keck Observatory

The next year, Andrea's group had only two nights to work with the telescope. The first night was not successful due to weather. But near the end of the second evening, they were able to take a clear photo.

With this image, the team plotted the orbit of several stars nearest to the Milky Way's center. They were closer to understanding the center of our galaxy.

SUCCESS

After years of observing the orbit of these stars, Andrea was able to show that stars near the center of the galaxy were orbiting a massive object that was not a visible star. The best explanation was that the stars were orbiting a super-massive black hole.

Ask & Answer

How is studying the center of the universe like solving a puzzle for Andrea?

ASTRONOMY

Andrea then tracked a star that went all the way around the center of the galaxy. This was a great boost to her research. The star is known as S2, and it takes only 15 years to move completely around the center of the Milky Way. In contrast, the sun takes 226 million years to orbit the Milky Way.

Based on the orbit of S2, Andrea calculated that the black hole has a mass 4 million times greater than our sun! What was her conclusion after more than a decade of research? That 26,000 light years from Earth, at the center of our galaxy, there exists a super-massive black hole.

"Become as broad as possible in your astronomical interests and become proficient in the tools you will need .... If you know your subject and are willing to work hard, you will be accepted."

—Carolyn Shoemaker, astronomer

Since her discovery, scientists have found super-massive black holes at the centers of most galaxies. We don't fully understand black holes yet, but Andrea's research is a significant step forward. It has also created new mysteries for her to solve. That, says Andrea, is what she loves about science.

HONORS AND AWARDS

Throughout her career, Andrea has received many awards for her contributions to science. In 2004, Andrea became the second-youngest scientist to be elected to the National Academy of Sciences. This is one of the highest honors for an American scientist. The same year, she was elected to the American Academy of Arts and Sciences. She has been called a leading figure among astrophysicists of her generation.

Andrea was named a 2008 MacArthur Fellow for her valuable work studying black holes in the evolution of galaxies. In 2012, Andrea became the first woman to receive the Crafoord Prize, one of the highest prizes in science. It was presented by the Royal Swedish Academy of Sciences for her work on black holes.

Galactic Center Group

Andrea is the director of the Galactic Center Group at UCLA. The Galactic Center Group is working to see deeper and deeper into space to learn about the black holes that lie at the centers of galaxies. You can learn more about the group's work and see pictures of what they study.

Galactic Center Group 🔍

Andrea on Screen

The public has come to know Andrea through popular media. She has given hundreds of talks, including presentations at the Aspen Center for Physics and a 2009 TED talk at Oxford, England. You can watch it here.

"Andrea Ghez" TED talk Oxford 🔍

Today, Andrea is the mother of two boys. She continues to teach at UCLA. Andrea is also continuing her research into the evolution of galaxies and is actively involved with the Thirty Meter Telescope (TMT) project.

Andrea has been on the TMT's science advisory committee since its first meeting more than 13 years ago. When built on Mauna Kea, the TMT will be the world's largest optical telescope. Astronomers will be able to see farther than ever before and test new theories. "It is truly amazing," says Andrea, "to think about what TMT will teach us about the universe."

"I like the risk of new technology. Maybe it won't work, but maybe it will open a fresh window on the universe, answering questions you didn't even know to ask."

—Andrea Ghez

ASK & ANSWER

Introduction

- Why is it important that both men and women pursue careers in astronomy? What would the science be like if only one gender worked in it?

Chapter 1

- If you lived in ancient times, what might you have thought when you saw an eclipse or a shooting star?

- Going into space is risky. How do space agencies and astronauts decide a mission is worth the risk? How do they make it as safe as possible?

- Are you interested in understanding our place in the universe? Do you get excited about Hubble images of other galaxies? Astronomy might be a good career for you.

Chapter 2

- What do you think Nancy was talking about when she called astronomy " the science of where you aren't?"

- Do you think it is important for women to have the same educational opportunities as men? Why or why not?

- Why do you think astronomers call our galaxy the Milky Way? What characteristics does it have that led to this name?

- Why is it sometimes hard to believe new information that goes against old information? Have you ever had to change how you think after learning something new?

- What does Nancy's experience with the press tell us about how women in the 1950s were treated differently than they are now?

- Nancy had several careers as an educator, researcher, and administrator. What does this tell you about how many jobs you may have in the future?

- Are awards and recognition important parts of a successful career? Would you be happy to do work you loved if you never received any special thank-you for it?

Chapter 3

- Has an event that happened in your lifetime sparked the same kind of excitement as the moon landing in 1969?

- How does your childhood affect the kind of person you are as a teenager? As an adult?

- What television programs or books have inspired you and why?

- Maggie turned her disappointment at her first telescope into a career. Have you ever been disappointed by the quality of something you saved up for? What did you do?

- Is education for kids only? Why is it important for adults to learn new things?

- Do you think there is intelligent life in outer space? Why or why not?

- How might science fiction inspire people to study science?

Chapter 4

- Can you think of other mysteries that exist in nature? Why do we find mysteries so fascinating?

- Can you remember what you wanted to be when you were younger? If so, has your choice of career changed or stayed the same and why do you think this is?

- Andrea encountered only one female science teacher during high school. How does this compare to your school? Would having more female science teachers in elementary and middle schools encourage more girls to study science?

- Andrea learned about black holes by observing things around them. Are there other things in nature that we can't see and have to study in this way?

- How is studying the center of the universe like solving a puzzle for Andrea?

Second Century

- Ptolemy claims the earth is the center of the universe.

Fourth Century

- Hypatia (350–415), an Egyptian woman, lectures on mathematics and astronomy and improves astronomical instruments.

Eleventh Century

- Hildegard of Bingen (1098–1179) develops a theory of a heliocentric solar system based on visions.

Sixteenth Century

- Nicolaus Copernicus (1473–1543) says all planets, including the earth, move around the sun.

Seventeenth Century

- Galileo Galilei (1564–1642) finds evidence of Copernicus' theories and is imprisoned until his death in 1642 for his ideas.

- Johannes Kepler (1571–1630) develops his three laws of planetary motion.

- Maria Cunitz (1610–1664) publishes a book called *Urania Propitia*, in which she translates and explains Johannes Kepler's work on planetary movement.

1702

- Maria Margarethe Kirch (1670–1720) becomes the first woman to discover a comet, although her husband takes credit for the discovery. She goes on to write several works on the aurora borealis and the planets Jupiter and Saturn.

1786

- Caroline Lucretia Herschel (1750–1848) discovers her first of eight comets and goes on to write two astronomical catalogues. She is given credit as the first woman to discover a comet.

1835

- Mary Somerville (1780–1872) and Caroline Herschel become the first women accepted into the Royal Astronomical Society.

1847

- Maria Mitchell (1818–1889) discovers a new comet with a telescope. In 1865, she becomes the first professor of astronomy at Vassar College.

1888

- Williamina Paton Stevens Fleming (1857–1911) discovers the Horse Nebulae. She classifies more than 10,000 stars while working at the Harvard College Observatory.

1893

- Henrietta Swan Leavitt (1868–1921) works at the Harvard College Observatory, where she creates the Harvard standard for measuring photographic magnitudes.

1922

- Annie Jump Cannon (1863–1941) creates a classification system for stars that is officially adopted by the International Astronomical Union.

1957

- Eleanor Margaret Burbidge (1919–) discovers that all elements, except the lightest, are produced in stars. She is the first woman to be appointed director of the Royal Greenwich Observatory.

1959

- Nancy Grace Roman (1925–) sets up NASA's astronomy program.

1967

- Jocelyn Bell Burnell (1943–) discovers the first radio pulsars.

1969

- Neil Armstrong (1930–2012) becomes the first person to walk on the moon.

1970s

- Vera Rubin (1928–) finds evidence to suggest that most of the mass in the universe is unseen. This mass is now called dark matter.

1983

- Sally Ride (1951–2012) becomes the first American woman in space.

1990s

- Carolyn C. Porco (1953–) leads an imaging team on the *Cassini* mission. This mission is still studying the Saturn system.

- Carolyn Shoemaker (1929–) is a co-discoverer of the comet Shoemaker-Levy 9.

2006

- Andrea Ghez (1965–) discovers a super-massive black hole in the center of the Milky Way.

2013

- Carolyn Porco arranges the famous picture from the *Cassini* spacecraft of Saturn and its rings, with Earth in the background, called "The Day the Earth Smiled."

aerospace: the technology and industry that deals with aviation and space flight.

asteroid: a small celestial body that revolves around the sun.

astrolabe: an instrument used to make astronomical measurements.

astronomer: a person who is an expert in the field of astronomy.

astronomical tables: an organized list of planetary information including the phases of the moon and eclipses.

astronomy: the science of the universe in which the stars, planets, and other astronomical bodies are studied.

astrophysics: a branch of physics that examines the physical and chemical processes of astronomical objects.

atmosphere: the blanket of gases around the earth.

atom: a small particle of matter.

BCE: put after a date, BCE stands for Before Common Era and counts down to zero. CE stands for Common Era and counts up from zero. The year this book is published is 2015 CE.

Big Dipper: a well-known group of seven stars in the northern sky.

binary stars: two stars that orbit one another or a common center.

black hole: an object whose gravitational field is so strong that even light cannot escape from it.

celestial: the sky or the universe.

circular: a disc-shaped object.

civil service: a branch of government that deals with administration.

classified: when something is grouped under specific headings.

climate change: a change in the earth's climate through a long period.

Cold War: a rivalry between the Soviet Union and the United States that began after World War II.

comet: a body in space believed to have a frozen center that orbits around the sun.

composition: the parts that make up something.

constellation: a group of stars that form a recognizable pattern.

crop: a plant grown for food and other uses.

culture: : a group of people and their beliefs and way of life.

data: information in the form of facts and numbers.

dense: tightly packed together.

dwarf planet: an astronomical object that orbits the sun that is smaller than a planet.

dyslexia: a learning problem that affects a person's ability to understand words, letters, or symbols.

eclipse: when the earth or the moon moves through the shadow of a celestial body.

electromagnetic: a force of the universe responsible for magnetic attraction and electrical charges.

element: a pure substance that is made of atoms that are all the same.

ellipse: an oval shape.

elliptical: an oval or egg-shaped object.

engineer: a person who uses science and math to design and build things.

ethnic: a large group of people who share a unique culture.

exoplanet: a planet that orbits a star other than the sun.

galactic plane: the plane that passes through the spiral arms of our galaxy.

galaxy: a vast amount of star systems held together by gravity.

gamma ray: light that has the shortest wavelength and highest energy.

gas: a substance in which atoms and molecules are spread far apart.

gender: male or female, and their roles or behavior defined by society.

gravitational pull: the force of an object that pulls objects toward it center.

gravity: a force that pulls two objects toward each other.

Great Depression: the worldwide economic crash from 1929 to 1939.

heat signature: the unique energy an object gives off.

heliocentric: a model of the universe in which the planets orbit the sun and the moon orbits the earth.

horizon: the line where the sky seems to meet the earth.

Hubble Space Telescope: a space telescope launched in 1990 into a low orbit around Earth.

International Space Station: a massive space station orbiting Earth.

intelligent life: living beings who have the ability to learn.

irrigate: when land is watered to help plants grow.

legend: a story handed down from one generation to the next.

light year: the distance (5.88 trillion miles or 9.46 trillion kilometers) that light travels in a solar year.

lunar: having to do with the moon.

lunar eclipse: when the moon's movement lines up the earth between the sun and the moon, casting the earth's shadow on the moon.

mass: the amount of matter an object has.

mathematics: a science that studies numbers, quantity, and space.

mechanical engineering: an area of engineering that deals with the design and construction of machines.

meridian: any line from the North Pole to the South Pole.

Middle Ages: a period in European history from about 350 to 1450.

Milky Way: the galaxy that contains our solar system.

molecule: a group of atoms bound together. Molecules combine to form matter.

myth: a story explaining a historical or natural event.

NASA: the National Aeronautics and Space Administration in charge of the American space program.

navigate: to plan a route.

nebula: a giant cloud of gas and dust among the stars.

observatory: a building with a telescope or other machines designed to observe objects in space.

optical: anything connected to light.

optics: an area of physics that studies how light behaves.

orbit: the path of an object circling another object in space.

Orion: a group of stars named for the son of an ancient god.

phenomena: an observed event.

photon: a tiny particle of light.

physicist: a scientist who studies matter, energy, and forces.

planetary motion: the way a planet moves.

Pleiades: a star cluster seen from almost anywhere on Earth.

Ptolemaic system: a model of the universe that places the earth at the center.

pulsar: a type of star that emits periodic radio waves, x-rays, and gamma rays.

radio astronomy: a field of astronomy that studies electromagnetic waves of radio frequency from outside the earth's atmosphere.

radio wave: an electromagnetic wave used for sending radio or television signals through the air.

reflecting telescope: a telescope that uses a mirror to gather and focus light.

Renaissance: a period in European history from the 1300s to the 1600s.

satellite: an object launched to orbit Earth. Also a celestial body that orbits a larger body.

sextant: a navigational instrument used to measure the angle between two objects, usually the horizon and a celestial body.

shooting star: a piece of rock called a meteoroid that burns up after falling into the earth's atmosphere.

solar: energy from the sun or having to do with the sun.

solar eclipse: when the moon passes between the sun and the earth, blocking the sun's light.

Space Race: a rivalry between the United States and the Soviet Union in the field of space exploration.

speckle imager: a method that produces high-resolution images.

spectroscope: an instrument used in science to measure wavelengths of light.

spectrum: a band of colors that a ray of light can be separated into to measure properties of the object, including motion and composition. Plural is spectra.

sphere: a perfectly round solid.

stereotype: a judgment about a group of individuals.

supernatural being: a being that has powers that the average person does not.

technology: the tools, methods, and systems used to solve a problem or do work.

telescope: an instrument used to observe distant objects.

ultraviolet light: a type of light with a shorter wavelength than visible light, also called black light.

universe: everything from planets and stars to all livings things, including you.

vertigo: a type of dizziness that causes you to lose your balance.

wavelength: the spacing of sound or light waves.

World War II: a world war fought from 1939 to 1945.

x-ray: a high-energy wave emitted by hot gases in the universe.

RESOURCES

Books

- Burleigh, Robert. *Look Up! Henrietta Leavitt, Pioneering Woman Astronomer.* Simon & Schuster/ Paula Wiseman Books, 2013.

- Croft, Malcolm. *Cool Astronomy: 50 Fantastic Facts for Kids of All Ages.* Pavilion, 2014.

- Ghez, Andrea, and Cohen, Judith Love. *You Can Be a Woman Astronomer.* Cascade Press, 1995.

- Lopez, Delano. *Amazing Solar System Projects You Can Build Yourself.* Nomad Press, 2008.

RESOURCES

Websites

- Cool Cosmos: *coolcosmos.ipac.caltech.edu*
- Engineer Girl: *engineergirl.org*
- European Space Agency-Kids: *esa.int/esaKIDSen*
- Lick Observatory: Ask an Astronomer: *ucolick.org/~mountain/AAA*
- NASA Space Place: *spaceplace.nasa.gov*
- Students for the Exploration and Development of Space: *seds.org*
- The Woman Astronomer: *womanastronomer.com*
- Women in Planetary Science: *womeninplanetaryscience.wordpress.com/profiles*

Museums and Planetariums

- Adler Planetarium: *www.adlerplanetarium.org*
- Hayden Planetarium-American Museum of Natural History: *www.amnh.org/our-research/hayden-planetarium*
- Intrepid Sea, Air, and Space Museum Complex: *www.intrepidmuseum.org*
- Morrison Planetarium at the California Academy of Sciences: *www.calacademy.org/exhibits/morrison-planetarium*
- National Air and Space Museum: *airandspace.si.edu*

QR Codes

- page 2 hubblesite.org/gallery
- page 11 time.com/3879943/lascaux-early-color-photos-of-the-famous-cave-paintings-france-1947
- page 12 mesopotamia.co.uk/astronomer/explore/exp_set.html
- page 13 loc.gov/exhibits/world/heavens.html
- page 16 nasa.gov/mp3/191322main_sputnik-beep.mp3
- page 19 kathrynauroragray.com
- page 20 zooniverse.org
- page 25 mariamitchell.org/research-and-collections/maria-mitchell/for-students
- page 26 brainpickings.org/2013/04/18/the-first-book-of-space-travel-jeanne-bendick/
- page 39 nationalcoldwarexhibition.org/schools-colleges/national-curriculum/space-race/nasa.aspx
- page 39 www.nasa.gov/50th/50th_magazine/coldWarCoOp.html
- page 41 hubblesite.org

RESOURCES

QR Codes (continued)

INDEX